AF265935

Chocolate Cake Delights

30 Amazing Chocolate Cake Recipes

By

Heston Brown

Copyright 2019 Heston Brown

All rights reserved. No part of this Book should be reproduced by any means including but not limited to: digital or mechanical copies, printed copies, scanning or photocopying unless approval is given by the Owner of the Book.

Any suggestions, guidelines or ideas in the Book are purely informative and the Author assumes no responsibility for any burden, loss, or damage caused by a misunderstanding of the information contained therein. The Reader assumes any and all risk when following information contained in the Book.

Thank you so much for buying my book! I want to give you a special gift!

Receive a special gift as a thank you for buying my book. Now you will be able to benefit from free and discounted book offers that are sent directly to your inbox every week.

To subscribe simply fill in the box below with your details and start reaping the rewards! A new deal will arrive every day and reminders will be sent so you never miss out. Fill in the box below to subscribe and get started!

https://heston-brown.getresponsepages.com

Subscribe
to our
newsletter

Your Email

Table of Contents

(1) Easy Flourless Chocolate Cake

This is an easy cake made without flour and can be served with whipping cream or with raspberries.

Cooking Time: 15 minutes.

Yield: 12.

List of Ingredients:

- Oil- 1 tsp.

- Semisweet chocolate- 15 ounces

- Unsalted butter- 15 ounces

- Sugar- 1 ¾ cup

- Eggs- 10

- Water- ¼ cup

- Vanilla extract- 2 tsp.

XXXXXXXXXXXXXXXXXXXXXXXXXXXXXXXXXXXXXXXXXXXXXXX

Instructions:

- Pre-heat your oven at 325 degrees Fahrenheit.

- Over a double boiler, melt the chocolate, butter and sugar.

- Cook for 5 minutes until smooth and melted.

- Cool the chocolate mixture.

- Once cooled, add in the eggs one by one.

- Now, add in the oil and the vanilla extract.

- Lastly, add the water.

- Mix all the ingredients and pour the mixture in to prepared pan and put to bake in preheated oven for about one hour or until the cake is done.

- Cool and serve!

(2) The Perfect Chocolate Cake

This moist and delicious chocolate cake is the perfect cake for all kinds of occasions and celebrations. Check out the recipe and try this perfect chocolate cake.

Cooking Time: 15 minutes.

Yield: 24

List of Ingredients:

- Flour- 2 cups

- Sugar- 2 cups

- Cocoa powder- ¾ cups

- Baking soda- 2 tsp.

- Baking powder- 1 tsp.

- Oil- ½ cup

- Milk- 1 cup

- Eggs- 2

- Vanilla extract- 1 tsp.

- Strong coffee- 1 cup

XXXXXXXXXXXXXXXXXXXXXXXXXXXXXXXXXXXXXXXXXXXXXXXXX

Instructions:

- Pre-heat your oven at 375 degrees Fahrenheit.

- In a bowl, mix the flour, sugar, cocoa powder, baking soda and baking powder.

- Now add in the oil, milk, eggs and the vanilla extract.

- Lastly, add in the cup of coffee.

- Mix properly.

- Pour the batter in to a prepared pan and put to bake in pre-heated oven for 25 to 30 minutes or until the cake is cooked.

(3) Crazy Chocolate Cake

 This chocolate cake is made on birthdays and is a favorite of kids.

Cooking Time: 20 minutes.

Yield: 18.

List of Ingredients:

- Flour- 3 cups

- Sugar- 2 cups

- Cocoa powder- 5/8 cup

- Salt- 1 tsp.

- Baking soda- 2 tsp.

- Vanilla extract- 1 tsp.

- Cold water- 2 cups

- White vinegar- 2 tsp.

- Oil- 2/3 cup

XXXXXXXXXXXXXXXXXXXXXXXXXXXXXXXXXXXXXXXXXXXXXXXXX

Instructions:

- Pre-heat your oven at 350 degrees Fahrenheit.

- In a bowl, mix the sugar, flour, salt, cocoa powder and baking soda.

- Make a well in the center and add in the vanilla extract, cold water, vinegar and oil.

- Mix all the ingredients well.

- Pour the batter into a prepared pan and put to bake in preheated oven for 35 minutes or until the cake is done.

(4) Chocolate Cake with Liquid Center

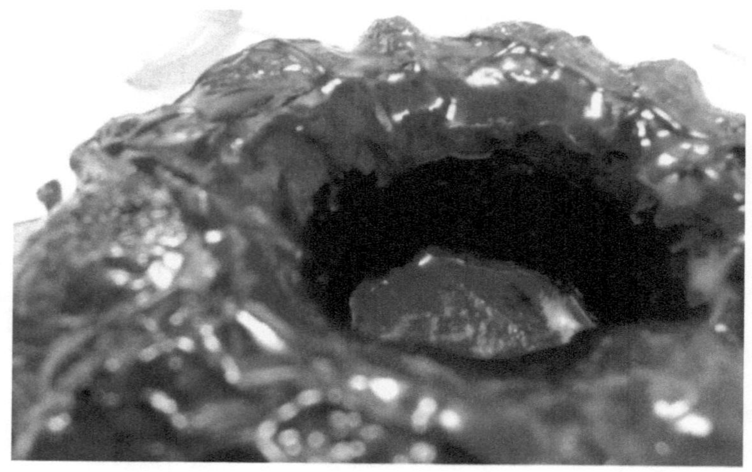

Use a bitter sweet chocolate for making this cake. This chocolate cake has a gooey and warm liquid in the center from which liquid oozes out when you cut it.

Cooking Time: 20 minutes.

Yield: 4.

List of Ingredients:

- Butter- ½ cup

- Bittersweet chocolate- 4 ounces

- Eggs- 2

- Egg yolks- 2

- Sugar- ¼ cup

- Flour- 2 tsp.

XXXXXXXXXXXXXXXXXXXXXXXXXXXXXXXXXXXXXXXXXXXXXXXX

Instructions:

- Pre-heat your oven at 450 degrees Fahrenheit.

- With the help of a double boiler, melt the butter and the chocolate until completely melted.

- In another bowl, beat the eggs, egg yolk and the sugar.

- Mix the egg mixture and the chocolate mixture and beat until just combined.

- Add the flour and mix.

- Pour the batter into greased ramekins and fill 3/4th of the ramekin.

- Bake for 6 to 7 minutes.

- Serve with ice cream or whipping cream.

(5) Moist Chocolate Cake

This moist chocolate cake is exceptionally yummy and is a must try for all the chocolate lovers out there.

Cooking Time: 20 minutes.

Yield: 24.

List of Ingredients:

- Mashed and cooked beets- 1.5 cups

- Vanilla extract- ½ tsp.

- Sugar- 1.5 cups

- Oil- 1 cup

- Eggs- 3

- Flour- 1 ¾ cups

- Baking soda- 1.5 tsp.

- Salt- ¼ tsp.

- Cocoa powder- 6 Tbsp.

XXXXXXXXXXXXXXXXXXXXXXXXXXXXXXXXXXXXXXXXXXXXXXXX

Instructions:

- Pre-heat your oven at 350 degrees Fahrenheit.

- In a bowl, mix the beets, eggs, vanilla extract, oil and the sugar.

- Now, add the flour, baking soda, salt and cocoa powder.

- Mix all the ingredients properly.

- Pour the batter in to prepared pan and put it to bake in preheated oven for about 25 to 30 minutes.

- Cool and serve!

(6) Molten Chocolate Cake with Sugar Coated Raspberries

The combination of chocolate and raspberries is very interesting and intimidating. This molten chocolate cake has a gooey center filling which is very tempting.

Cooking Time: 20 minutes.

Yield: 8.

List of Ingredients:

- Unsalted butter- 1 cup
- Semisweet chocolate chips- 8 ounces
- Eggs- 5
- Sugar- ½ cup
- Salt- a pinch
- Flour- 4 tsp.
- Muffin cups- 8
- Raspberries- 6 ounces
- Sugar- ½ cup

XXXXXXXXXXXXXXXXXXXXXXXXXXXXXXXXXXXXXXXXXXXXXXXXX

Instructions:

- Pre-heat your oven at 475 degrees Fahrenheit.

- Melt the chocolate and the butter in a pan.

- In a bowl, beat the eggs, sugar and salt.

- Mix the egg mixture with the chocolate mixture.

- Now, add in the flour and mix.

- Pour the mixture into the muffin cups and put to bake in preheated oven.

- Bake for 7 to 8 minutes.

- Before serving, dust with sugar and raspberries.

(7) Coconut Chocolate Cake

Moist and delicious with the flavors of coconut this cake is a must try.

Cooking Time: 15 minutes.

Yield: 16.

List of Ingredients:

- Chocolate fudge cake mix- 18.25 ounce

- Butter- 2 Tbsp.

- Evaporated milk- ½ cup

- Marshmallows- 25

- Flaked coconut- 14 ounces

- Chocolate fudge frosting- 16-ounce container

XXXXXXXXXXXXXXXXXXXXXXXXXXXXXXXXXXXXXXXXXXXXX

Instructions:

- Prepare the chocolate cake fudge mix according to the instructions on the package.

- For the frosting, melt the butter in a sauce pan.

- Add in the evaporated milk.

- Now, add in the marshmallows and mix to melt.

- Stir in the flaked coconut

- Assemble the cake.

- Frost first with the coconut frosting.

- Now, frost the sides of the cake with the chocolate fudge frosting.

(8) Sugar Free Molten Cake

Right from the oven, these molten cakes are the best cakes that are actually delicious. Apart from that they are even sugar free so you need not worry about the calories as well.

Cooking Time: 5 minutes.

Yield: 4.

List of Ingredients:

- Unsweetened chocolate- 4 ounces

- Unsalted butter- ½ cup

- Eggs- 2

- Egg yolks- 2

- Stevia blend- ¼ cup

- Flour- 2 Tbsp.

- Salt- a pinch

- Whipping cream- ½ cup

XXXXXXXXXXXXXXXXXXXXXXXXXXXXXXXXXXXXXXXXXXXXXX

Instructions:

- Pre-heat your oven at 400 degrees Fahrenheit.

- With the help of a double boiler, melt the chocolate and the butter.

- In another bowl, mix the eggs, egg yolks, stevia blend, flour and the salt.

- Add the chocolate mixture in the egg mixture and mix well.

- Pour the batter in to greased ramekins and put in the preheated oven to bake for about 7 to 8 minutes.

- Whip the cream until soft peaks form.

- Serve the molten cake with a dollop of whipping cream.

(9) Mexican Chocolate Cake

This Mexican chocolate cake is made with a dash of cinnamon which makes it different from the other chocolate cakes.

Cooking Time: 15 minutes.

Yield: 36.

List of Ingredients:

- Flour- 2 cups

- Cocoa powder- ¼ cup

- Sugar- 2 cups

- Baking soda- 1 tsp.

- Cinnamon- 1 tsp.

- Softened margarine- ½ cup

- Oil- ½ cup

- Water- 1 cup

- Sour milk- ½ cup

- Eggs- 2

- Vanilla extract- 1 tsp.

XXXXXXXXXXXXXXXXXXXXXXXXXXXXXXXXXXXXXXXXXXXXXXXX

Instructions:

- Pre-heat your oven at 350 degrees Fahrenheit.

- In a bowl, mix the flour, cocoa powder, sugar, baking soda and the cinnamon.

- Set aside.

- In another bowl, beat the margarine and the eggs.

- Add in the oil and the vanilla extract.

- Now, add the sour milk alternating it with the flour mixture.

- Lastly, add in the water and mix properly.

- Pour the batter in to prepared pan and put to bake for 25 to 30 minutes or until the cake is done.

(10) Too Much Chocolaty Cake

True to its name, this cake is extremely chocolaty and one piece of it is never enough.

Cooking Time: 20 minutes.

Yield: 12.

List of Ingredients:

- Devil's food cake mix- 1 package
- Instant chocolate pudding mix- 6 ounces
- Sour cream- 1 cup
- Vegetable oil- 1 cup
- Eggs- 4
- Water- ½ cup
- Semisweet chocolate chips- 2 cups

xxxxxxxxxxxxxxxxxxxxxxxxxxxxxxxxxxxxxxxxxxxxxxxxx

Instructions:

- Preheat your oven at 375 degrees Fahrenheit.
- In a bowl, mix together the devil's food cake mix, instant pudding mix, sour cream, vegetable oil, eggs and the water.
- Mix properly and then fold the chocolate chips.
- Pour the batter in to a prepared pan and put to bake in preheated oven for 50 to 55 minutes or until cake is done.
- Serve!

(11) Moms Chocolate Cake

This cake bakes up really high and fluffy and can be easily made.

Cooking Time: 15 minutes.

Yield: 24.

List of Ingredients:

- Sugar- 2 cups
- Shortening- ½ cup
- Eggs- 2
- Cocoa powder- ¾ cup
- Milk- 1 cup
- Flour- 2 cups
- Baking powder- 1.5 tsp.
- Brewed hot coffee- 1 cup
- Baking soda- 2 tsp.
- Vanilla extract- 2.5 tsp.

XXXXXXXXXXXXXXXXXXXXXXXXXXXXXXXXXXXXXXXXXXXXXXXXXX

Instructions:

- Pre-heat your oven at 350 degrees Fahrenheit.

- In a bowl, beat the shortening and the sugar until light and fluffy.

- Add in the eggs and mix well.

- Now, add in the cocoa powder, milk, flour, baking powder, baking soda and the vanilla extract.

- Mix well.

- Pour the mixture in to prepared pan and put to bake in pre-heated oven for 30 to 35 minutes or until the cake is done.

- Cool and serve!

(12) German Sweet Chocolate Cake

This chocolate cake with a coconut and pecan frosting is the perfect cake one would want to eat.

Cooking Time:40 minutes.

Yield: 24.

List of Ingredients:

- German sweet chocolate- 4 ounces
- Water- ½ cup
- Flour- 2 cups
- Baking soda- 1 tsp.
- Salt- ¼ tsp.
- Softened butter- 1 cup
- Sugar- 2 cups
- Egg yolks- 4
- Vanilla extract- 1 tsp.
- Buttermilk- 1 cup
- Egg whites- 4
- Evaporated milk- 12 ounces
- Sugar- 1.5 cups
- Butter- ¾ cup
- Egg yolks- 4
- Vanilla extract- 1.5 tsp.
- Flaked coconut- 8 ounces
- Chopped pecans- 1.5 cups

Instructions:

- Pre-heat your oven at 375 degrees Fahrenheit.

- Melt the chocolate with the water in the microwave.

- Mix flour, baking soda and the salt in a bowl.

- In another bowl, beat the butter and the sugar.

- Add in the egg yolks one by one and mix.

- Now, add in the vanilla extract and the chocolate.

- Now, add in the flour mixture alternating it with the buttermilk.

- In another bowl, beat egg whites and fold in the cake mixture.

- Mix and pour the batter in to prepared pan and put to bake in preheated oven for 30 minutes.

- Frost with the German frosting and then serve!

(13) Swedish Sticky Chocolate Cake

This is a Swedish recipe of a chocolate cake and it is also known as Kladdkaka which means sticky chocolate cake.

Cooking Time: 10 minutes.

Yield: 8.

List of Ingredients:

- Flour- ½ cup

- Cocoa powder- ¼ cup

- Salt- a pinch

- Eggs- 2

- Sugar- 1 1/3 cup

- Vanilla extract- 1 Tbsp.

- Melted butter- ½ cup

xxxxxxxxxxxxxxxxxxxxxxxxxxxxxxxxxxxxxxxxxxxxxxxxx

Instructions:

- Pre-heat your oven at 300 degrees Fahrenheit.

- Sift the cocoa powder, flour and salt.

- Beat the eggs and the sugar.

- Add in the flour mixture and mix.

- Now, add the vanilla extract and melted butter and mix properly.

- Pour the batter in to a prepared pie plate and put to bake in preheated oven for 35 minutes.

- Let it cool and refrigerate for the night and then serve cold!

(14) German Chocolate Cake Frosting

German chocolate frosting is done on the German chocolate cake while it's warm. This German chocolate frosting adds to the taste of the German chocolate cake.

Cooking Time: 15 minutes.

Yield: 12.

List of Ingredients:

- Evaporated milk- 1 cup
- White sugar- 1 cup
- Egg yolks- 3
- Margarine- ½ cup
- Vanilla extract- 1 tsp.
- Chopped pecans- 1 cup
- Flaked coconut- 1 cup

XXXXXXXXXXXXXXXXXXXXXXXXXXXXXXXXXXXXXXXXXXXXXXX

Instructions:

- In a sauce pan, add the evaporated milk, egg yolks, sugar, margarine and the vanilla extract.
- Stir and mix to combine.
- Remove from heat and add in the chopped pecans and the flaked coconut.
- Spread over warm cake and serve!

(15) Victory Chocolate Cake

This cake dates back as far as the World War 2 when there was a shortage of sugar supply in the city.

Cooking Time:20 minutes.

Yield: 24.

List of Ingredients:

- Flour- 2 cups

- Baking soda- 2 ¼ tsp.

- Shortening- ¾ cup

- Dark corn syrup- 1 ½ cup

- Vanilla extract- 1.5 tsp.

- Cocoa powder- ½ cup

- Salt- ¾ tsp.

- Sugar- 1/3 cup

- Eggs- 3

- Cold brewed coffee- 1 cup

XXXXXXXXXXXXXXXXXXXXXXXXXXXXXXXXXXXXXXXXXXXXXXXXXXXX

Instructions:

- Pre-heat oven at 350 degrees Fahrenheit.

- Mix together the flour, cocoa powder, salt and baking soda.

- In another bowl, beat the shortening and the sugar.

- Now, add in the egg yolks and the corn syrup.

- Now, add the cold brewed coffee alternating it with the dry ingredients.

- In another bowl, beat the egg whites until soft peaks form.

- Fold the egg whites in the cake mixture and mix properly.

- Pour the batter in to prepared pans and put to bake in preheated oven for 45 minutes or until the cake is done.

- Cool and serve!

(16) Extreme Chocolate Cake

This is the best chocolate cake in the world because of the rich chocolate flavor and the butter cream icing.

Cooking Time: 30 minutes.

Yield: 12.

List of Ingredients:

- Sugar- 2 cups

- Flour- 1 ¾ cups

- Cocoa powder- ¾ cup

- Salt- 1 tsp.

- Baking soda- 1 ½ tsp.

- Eggs- 2

- Baking powder- 1 ½ tsp.

- Milk- 1 cup

- Oil- ½ cup

- Boiling water- 1 cup

- Vanilla extract- 2 tsp.

- Butter- ¾ cup

- Cocoa powder- 1.5 cups

- Confectioners' sugar- 5 cups

- Milk- 2/3 cup

- Vanilla extract- 1 tsp.

xxxxxxxxxxxxxxxxxxxxxxxxxxxxxxxxxxxxxxxxxxxxxxxxxx

Instructions:

- Pre-heat your oven at 375 degrees Fahrenheit.

- In a bowl, mix the cocoa powder, flour, baking powder, sugar, baking soda and the salt.

- Now, add in the milk, eggs, oil and the vanilla extract and mix properly.

- Now, add in the boiling water and mix properly.

- Pour the batter into a greased pan and put to bake in preheated oven for about 30-35 minutes or until the cake is done.

- For frosting, beat the butter and add in the cocoa powder, confectioner's sugar, vanilla extract and the milk.

- Mix until it is the type of frosting you want.

- Add more milk if required.

- Frost on the cake once cooled!

(17) Dark German Chocolate Cake

This is a dark German chocolate cake which is to die for.

Cooking Time: 15 minutes.

Yield: 12.

List of Ingredients:

- Sugar- 3 cups
- Flour- 2 ¾ cups
- Cocoa powder- 1 cup plus 2 Tbsp.
- Baking soda- 2 tsp.
- Baking powder- 2 tsp.
- Salt- 1 tsp.
- Milk- 1.5 cups
- Oil- ¾ cup
- Eggs- 3
- Vanilla extract- 1 Tbsp.
- Hot water- 1.5 cups

XXXXXXXXXXXXXXXXXXXXXXXXXXXXXXXXXXXXXXXXXXXXXXX

Instructions:

- In a bowl, mix the sugar, flour, cocoa powder, baking soda, baking powder and the salt. Set aside.

- Now, add in the milk, oil, eggs and the vanilla extract.

- Lastly, add in the boiling water and mix well.

- Pour the batter into a prepared pan and put to bake in preheated oven for 25 to 30 minutes or until cake is done.

- Cool and serve!

(18) Flourless Chocolate Cake

This is a dense chocolate cake for those who do not wish to consume wheat or gluten.

Cooking Time:20 minutes.

Yield: 16.

List of Ingredients:

- Water- ½ cup

- Salt- ¼ tsp.

- Sugar- ¾ cup

- Bittersweet chocolate- 18 squares

- Unsalted butter- 1 cup

- Eggs- 6

XXXXXXXXXXXXXXXXXXXXXXXXXXXXXXXXXXXXXXXXXXXXXXXX

Instructions:

- Preheat your oven at 300 degrees Fahrenheit.

- In a sauce pan, add the water, salt and the sugar and mix until dissolved.

- Melt the bittersweet chocolate in the microwave.

- Beat the butter with the melted chocolate and slowly add in the water mixture.

- Now, add the eggs one by one.

- Pour the batter in to a prepared pan and put to bake in preheated oven for 45 minutes.

- Serve!

(19) Easy Chocolate Cake

This is the easiest chocolate cake in the world with very simple ingredients and easy to make.

Cooking Time: 20 minutes.

Yield: 24.

List of Ingredients:

- Sugar- 2 cups

- Flour- 1 ¾ cups

- Cocoa powder- ¾ cup

- Baking powder- 1.5 tsp.

- Baking soda- 1.5 tsp.

- Salt- 1 tsp.

- Eggs- 2

- Milk- 1 cup

- Oil- ½ cup

- Vanilla extract- 2 tsp.

- Boiling water- 1 cup

xxxxxxxxxxxxxxxxxxxxxxxxxxxxxxxxxxxxxxxxxxxxxxxxxxx

Instructions:

- Pre-heat your oven at 350 degrees Fahrenheit.

- In a large bowl, mix the flour, sugar, cocoa powder, baking powder, baking soda and the salt.

- In the center, add in the eggs, milk, oil and the vanilla extract.

- Lastly, add in the boiling water.

- Beat well and pour the batter into a prepared pan and put to bake in preheated oven for 30 to 35 minutes or until the cake is done.

- Cool and serve!

(20) One Bowl Chocolate Cake

This cake is very moist and delicious to eat. It is very simple and easy to make.

Cooking Time:20 minutes.

Yield: 24.

List of Ingredients:

- Sugar- 2 cups
- Flour- 1 ¾ cups
- Cocoa powder- ¾ cup
- Baking powder- 1.5 tsp.
- Baking soda- 1.5 tsp.
- Salt- 1 tsp.
- Eggs- 2
- Milk- 1 cup
- Oil- ½ cup
- Vanilla extract- 2 tsp.
- Boiling water- 1 cup

XXXXXXXXXXXXXXXXXXXXXXXXXXXXXXXXXXXXXXXXXXXXXXX

Instructions:

- Pre-heat your oven at 375 degrees Fahrenheit.

- In a bowl, mix the sugar, cocoa powder, flour, baking soda, baking powder and the salt.

- Now, add in the eggs, milk, oil and the vanilla extract.

- Finally, add in the boiling water.

- Then the batter will be thin.

- Pour the batter into a prepared pan and put to bake in preheated oven for 35 minutes or until done.

- Serve once cool!

(21) No Fail Chocolate Cake

 As the name suggests, this chocolate cake is very easy to make and the recipe is absolutely fool proof so you will not be having any problems in making it.

Cooking Time: 10 minutes.

Yield: 48.

List of Ingredients:

- Butter- 1 cup

- Sugar- 2 cups

- Eggs- 2

- Buttermilk- 1 cup

- Cocoa powder- ½ cup

- Flour- 2.5 cups

- Baking soda- 2 tsp.

- Salt- ½ tsp.

- Boiling water- 1 cup

xxxxxxxxxxxxxxxxxxxxxxxxxxxxxxxxxxxxxxxxxxxxxxxx

Instructions:

- Pre-heat your oven at 350 degrees Fahrenheit.

- Mix together the cocoa powder, flour, baking soda and the salt.

- In a bowl, beat the sugar and butter with the until fluffy and light.

- Add in the eggs one at a time,

- Now, add the buttermilk alternating with the flour mixture.

- Lastly, add the boiling water.

- Pour the batter in to a prepared pan and put to bake in preheated oven for 30-40 minutes or until the cake is done.

- Serve once cool!

(22) Nairobi Chocolate Cake

This is a Kenyan recipe of chocolate cake and is very delicious.

Cooking Time:20 minutes

Yield: 8.

List of Ingredients:

- Flour- 2 cups
- Baking soda- 1 tsp.
- Baking powder- ½ tsp.
- Sugar- 1 ¾ cups
- Salt- 1 tsp.
- Cocoa powder- ¾ cup
- Water- ¾ cup
- Oil- ¾ cup
- Eggs- 3
- Vanilla extract- 1 tsp.
- Water- ½ cup

XXXXXXXXXXXXXXXXXXXXXXXXXXXXXXXXXXXXXXXXXXXXXXXXXX

Instructions:

- Pre-heat your oven at 350 degrees Fahrenheit.

- In a bowl, mix the flour, baking soda, baking powder, sugar, salt, cocoa powder and the water.

- Now, add in the oil and beat.

- Add in the eggs and the vanilla extract.

- Add the half cup of water and mix properly.

- Pour the batter in to prepared pans and put to bake in preheated oven for about 30 minutes or until the cake is done.

(23) Cherry Chocolate Cake

This cake is a favorite of those who love cherries and the combination of chocolate and cherry makes it more tempting to eat.

Cooking Time: 15 minutes.

Yield: 24.

List of Ingredients:

- Butter- ½ cup

- Sugar- 1.5 cups

- Eggs- 2

- Almond extract- 1 tsp.

- Cocoa powder- ½ cup

- Cake flour- 1 ¾ cups

- Baking soda- 2 tsp.

- Salt- 1 tsp.

- Cherry pie filling- 21 ounces

XXXXXXXXXXXXXXXXXXXXXXXXXXXXXXXXXXXXXXXXXXXXXXX

Instructions:

- Pre-heat your oven at 350 degrees Fahrenheit.

- Beat the butter and sugar till they are fluffy.

- Now, add in the eggs and the almond extract.

- Add the cocoa powder and mix.

- Add the cake flour, baking soda and the salt.

- Stir in the cherry pie filling.

- Mix and pour the batter in to prepared pan and put to bake in pre-heated oven for 30 to 35 minutes or until the cake is done.

- Serve!

(24) Perfect Chocolate Cake

This is an incredibly moist and rich cake with a whipped cream filling along with a chocolate butter cream frosting.

Cooking Time: 30 minutes.

Yield: 12.

List of Ingredients:

- Cocoa powder- 1 cup
- Boiling water- 2 cups
- Flour- 2 ¾ cups
- Baking soda- 2 tsp.
- Salt- ½ tsp.
- Baking powder- ½ tsp.
- Softened butter- 1 cup
- Sugar- 2 ½ cups
- Eggs- 4
- Vanilla extract- 1.5 tsp.
- Cream- 1 pint
- Confectioners' sugar- 1 cup
- Vanilla extract- 1 tsp.
- Cocoa powder- 2 Tbsp.

xxxxxxxxxxxxxxxxxxxxxxxxxxxxxxxxxxxxxxxxxxxxxxxxxxx

Instructions:

- Pre-heat your oven at 350 degrees Fahrenheit.

- Mix the cocoa powder and the boiling water and mix.

- In another bowl, mix the flour, baking soda, salt and the baking powder.

- Mix the butter and the sugar and add in the eggs one at a time.

- Now add in the vanilla extract.

- Now add the dry ingredients alternating with the cocoa powder mixture.

- Mix properly and pour the batter into a prepared pan and put to bake in preheated oven for 20 minutes or until the cake is done.

- For the topping, whip the cream with vanilla extract.

- Add in the confectioners' sugar and spread on top of the cake.

- For the frosting, beat the butter, sugar, vanilla extract and the cocoa powder.

- Frost the cake once it's cooled.

- Serve!

(25) Black Chocolate Cake

This is a rich black chocolate cake with lots of cocoa powder and sugar.

Cooking Time: 10 minutes.

Yield: 12.

List of Ingredients:

- Flour- 2 cups
- Sugar- 2 cups
- Baking soda- 2 tsp.
- Baking powder- 2 tsp.
- Cocoa powder- 1 cup
- Salt- a pinch
- Shortening- 2/3 cup
- Boiling water- 2 cups
- Eggs- 2
- Vanilla extract- 2 tsp.

XXXXXXXXXXXXXXXXXXXXXXXXXXXXXXXXXXXXXXXXXXXXXXXX

Instructions:

- Pre-heat your oven at 350 degrees Fahrenheit.

- Mix the flour, cocoa powder, sugar, baking soda, baking powder and the salt.

- Mix the boiling water and the shortening and add to the flour mixture.

- Now, add in the eggs and the vanilla extract.

- Mix and pour the batter in to a prepared pan and put to bake in preheated oven for 30 minutes or until the cake is done.

(26) French Chocolate Cake

This is a typical French style chocolate cake made with dense chocolate and served with whipped cream.

Cooking Time: 35 minutes.

Yield: 12.

List of Ingredients:

- Sugar- ½ cup
- Semisweet chocolate- 10 squares
- Unsalted butter- ¾ cup
- Vanilla extract- 2 tsp.
- Eggs, separated- 5
- Flour- ¼ cup
- Tartar- a pinch
- Salt- a pinch
- Confectioners' sugar- for dusting

XXXXXXXXXXXXXXXXXXXXXXXXXXXXXXXXXXXXXXXXXXXXXXXX

Instructions:

- Pre-heat your oven at 325 degrees Fahrenheit.

- In a sauce pan, add the butter, chocolate and 3/4th of the sugar and let it melt and mix.

- Remove from heat and add in the vanilla extract.

- Add in egg yolks once the mixture has cooled.

- Now, add the flour.

- In another bowl, beat the egg whites until they turn foamy and add in the tartar and the salt and continue to beat.

- Now, add in the remaining sugar in the egg whites.

- Fold in the egg white mixture in chocolate mixture.

- Pour the batter in to ready pan and bake for about 45 minutes or until cake is done.

- Cool, dust with sugar and serve!

(27) Gluten Free Chocolate Cake

This is a fudgy and moist chocolate cake which is gluten free. The quinoa added is a big surprise and makes it more delicious.

Cooking Time: 15 minutes.

Yield: 10.

List of Ingredients:

- Water- 1 1/3 cups

- Quinoa- 2/3 cup

- Melted butter- ¾ cup

- Milk- 1/3 cup

- Eggs- 4

- Vanilla extract- 1 tsp.

- Sugar- 1.5 cups

- Cocoa powder- 1 cup

- Baking powder- 1.5 tsp.

- Baking soda- ½ tsp.

- Salt- ½ tsp.

XXXXXXXXXXXXXXXXXXXXXXXXXXXXXXXXXXXXXXXXXXXXXXXX

Instructions:

- In a sauce pan, boil the water and the quinoa.

- Simmer for a few minutes and let it cook.

- Pre-heat your oven at 350 degrees Fahrenheit.

- In a blender, blend the butter, eggs, milk, and vanilla extract.

- Now, add in the softened quinoa.

- Now, add in the sugar, cocoa powder, baking powder, baking soda and the salt and mix.

- Pour the batter in to a prepared pan and put to bake in preheated oven for 40 to 45 minutes or until the cake is done.

- Serve!

(28) Old Fashioned Cake

This cake is same as that kind which was made in the olden days.

Cooking Time: 45 minutes.

Yield: 18.

List of Ingredients:

- Butter- 1 cup
- Water- 1 cup
- Cocoa powder- 4 Tbsp.
- Buttermilk- ½ cup
- Baking soda- 1 tsp.
- Eggs- 2
- Vanilla extract- 1 tsp.
- Flour- 2 cups
- Sugar- 2 cups
- Ground cinnamon- 1 tsp.
- Salt- ½ tsp.
- Butter- ½ cup
- Cocoa powder- 4 Tbsp.
- Buttermilk- 1/3 cup
- Confectioners' sugar- 4 cups
- Vanilla extract- 1 tsp.
- Pecans- 1 cup
- Salt- a pinch

XXXXXXXXXXXXXXXXXXXXXXXXXXXXXXXXXXXXXXXXXXXXXXX

Instructions:

- Pre-heat your oven at 350 degrees Fahrenheit.

- In a sauce pan, melt the butter, water and the cocoa powder and mix.

- In another bowl, mix the baking soda, buttermilk, eggs and the vanilla.

- Stir this mixture in to the cooled cocoa mixture.

- In another bowl, mix the flour, sugar, cinnamon and salt.

- Add in the dry ingredients in the cocoa mixture.

- Pour the batter in to prepared pan and put to bake in pre-heated oven for 30 minutes or until the cake is done.

- For the frosting, beat the butter, cocoa powder, buttermilk, confectioners' sugar, vanilla extract and the salt.

- Fold in the pecans and frost over the cooled cake.

(29) Black Magic Cake

This chocolate cake is super chocolaty and suitable for all kinds of night time parties.

Cooking Time: 15 minutes.

Yield: 24.

List of Ingredients:

- Flour- 1 ¾ cups

- Sugar- 2 cups

- Cocoa powder- ¾ cup

- Baking soda- 2 tsp.

- Baking powder- 1 tsp.

- Salt- 1 tsp.

- Eggs- 2

- Brewed coffee- 1 cup

- Buttermilk- 1 cup

- Oil- ½ cup

- Vanilla extract- 1 tsp.

XXXXXXXXXXXXXXXXXXXXXXXXXXXXXXXXXXXXXXXXXXXXXXXX

Instructions:

- Pre-heat your oven at 350 degrees Fahrenheit.

- In a bowl, mix the flour, sugar, cocoa powder, baking powder, baking soda and salt.

- Now, add the eggs, brewed coffee, buttermilk, oil and the vanilla extract.

- Beat well and pour the mixture in to prepared pan and put it to bake in preheated oven for 30 minutes or until cake is done.

- Serve!

(30) Chocolate Amaretto Lava Cakes

Served with a dollop of whipped cream and a center gooey filling of chocolate amaretto these molten lava cakes are a must try.

Cooking Time:20 minutes.

Yield: 6.

List of Ingredients:

- Bittersweet chocolate- 1 cup
- Whipping cream- ¼ cup
- Amaretto- 3 Tbsp.
- Butter- ½ cup
- Eggs- 2
- Egg yolks- 2
- Sugar- 1/3 cup
- Cake flour- ¼ cup

xxxxxxxxxxxxxxxxxxxxxxxxxxxxxxxxxxxxxxxxxxxxxxxxxx

Instructions:

- Melt 1/3 of the chocolate and the whipping cream.

- Add in half of the amaretto.

- Freeze the mixture for one hour and then form balls from it.

- For the cake, melt the remaining chocolate and the butter.

- Remove from heat and add the rest of the amaretto and set aside.

- In another bowl, mix the eggs and the egg yolks.

- Add in the sugar and beat.

- Fold in the chocolate mixture and add in the cake flour.

- Pour this mixture in to each ramekin.

- Now, gently press one ball in the center of the mixture in the ramekins.

- Bake for 15 minutes or until the cake is done.

- Serve with whipped cream!

About the Author

Heston Brown is an accomplished chef and successful e-book author from Palo Alto California. After studying cooking at The New England Culinary Institute, Heston stopped briefly in Chicago where he was offered head chef at some of the city's most prestigious restaurants. Brown decide that he missed the rolling hills and sunny weather of California and moved back to his home state to open up his own catering company and give private cooking classes.

Heston lives in California with his beautiful wife of 18 years and his two daughters who also have aspirations to follow in their father's footsteps and pursue careers in the culinary arts. Brown is well known for his delicious fish and chicken dishes and teaches these recipes as well as many others to his students.

When Heston gave up his successful chef position in Chicago and moved back to California, a friend suggested he use the internet to share his recipes with the world and so he did! To date, Heston Brown has written over 1000 e-books that contain recipes, cooking tips, business strategies for catering companies and a self-help book he wrote from personal experience.

He claims his wife has been his inspiration throughout many of his endeavours and continues to be his partner in business as well as life. His greatest joy is having all three women in his life in the kitchen with him cooking their favourite meal while his favourite jazz music plays in the background.

Author's Afterthoughts

Thank you to all the readers who invested time and money into my book! I cherish every one of you and hope you took the same pleasure in reading it as I did in writing it.

Out of all of the books out there, you chose mine and for that I am truly grateful. It makes the effort worth it when I know my readers are enjoying my work from beginning to end.

Please take a few minutes to write an Amazon review so that others can benefit from your opinions and insight. Your review will help countless other readers make an informed choice

Thank you so much,

Heston Brown

www.ingramcontent.com/pod-product-compliance
Lightning Source LLC
Chambersburg PA
CBHW031322060726
47590CB00003B/1306